The Smart & Easy Guide To Selling: Sell Anything To Anyone With These Proven Sales Techniques, Planning, Analysis, Training, Coaching, Confidence, Management & Leadership Strategies

Vince Cooper

Legal Stuff

Copyright Information

Copyright © 2013 Checkmate Marketing Group LLC. All rights reserved worldwide.

No part of this publication may be replicated, redistributed, or given away in any form without the prior written consent of the publisher.

Checkmate Marketing Group LLC

Earnings Disclaimer

EVERY EFFORT HAS BEEN MADE TO ACCURATELY REPRESENT THIS PRODUCT AND IT'S POTENTIAL. IN TERMS OF EARNINGS, THERE IS NO GUARANTEE THAT YOU WILL EARN ANY MONEY USING THE TECHNIQUES AND IDEAS IN THIS MATERIAL. INFORMATION PRESENTED ON THIS BOOK IS NOT TO BE INTERPRETED AS A PROMISE OR GUARANTEE OF EARNINGS. EARNING POTENTIAL IS ENTIRELY DEPENDENT ON THE PERSON USING OUR PRODUCT, IDEAS AND TECHNIQUES.

ANY CLAIMS MADE OF ACTUAL EARNINGS OR EXAMPLES OF ACTUAL RESULTS CAN BE VERIFIED UPON REQUEST. YOUR LEVEL OF SUCCESS IN ATTAINING THE RESULTS CLAIMED IN OUR MATERIALS DEPENDS ON THE TIME YOU DEVOTE TO THE PROGRAM, IDEAS AND TECHNIQUES MENTIONED, YOUR FINANCES, KNOWLEDGE AND VARIOUS SKILLS. SINCE THESE FACTORS DIFFER ACCORDING TO INDIVIDUALS, WE CANNOT GUARANTEE YOUR SUCCESS OR INCOME LEVEL.

ANY AND ALL FORWARD LOOKING STATEMENTS HERE OR ON ANY OF OUR SALES MATERIAL ARE INTENDED TO EXPRESS OUR OPINION OF EARNINGS POTENTIAL. MANY FACTORS WILL BE IMPORTANT IN DETERMINING YOUR ACTUAL RESULTS AND NO GUARANTEES ARE MADE THAT YOU WILL ACHIEVE RESULTS SIMILAR TO OURS OR ANYONE ELSES. NO GUARANTEES ARE MADE THAT YOU WILL ACHIEVE ANY RESULTS FROM OUR IDEAS AND TECHNIQUES IN OUR MATERIAL.

Limitation of Liability

THE MATERIALS IN THIS BOOK ARE PROVIDED "AS IS" WITHOUT ANY EXPRESS OR IMPLIED WARRANTY OF ANY KIND INCLUDING WARRANTIES OF MERCHANTABILITY, NONINFRINGEMENT OF INTELLECTUAL PROPERTY, OR FITNESS FOR ANY PARTICULAR PURPOSE. IN NO EVENT SHALL OR ITS AGENTS OR OFFICERS BE LIABLE FOR ANY DAMAGES WHATSOEVER (INCLUDING, WITHOUT LIMITATION, DAMAGES FOR LOSS OF PROFITS, BUSINESS INTERRUPTION, LOSS OF INFORMATION, INJURY OR DEATH) ARISING OUT OF THE USE OF OR INABILITY TO USE THE MATERIALS, EVEN IF HAS BEEN ADVISED OF THE POSSIBILITY OF SUCH LOSS OR DAMAGES.

Table of Contents

Introduction 6
Where do we begin? 11
Egoist and egotist 13
Compare your list with mine 15
Common automatic negative thoughts that keep you from being an effective salesperson 30
Defining need: inner motivations for buying activities 38
What should you sell? 44
A true story that I hope will inspire you 46
What lesson can you learn from her story? 49
We Want Your Feedback on This Book! 52

Introduction

I remember my son coming home from school one day deep in thought and holding out to me a slip of paper. It was the result of his skills and aptitude assessment which should help him determine what further education path to take after high school. He showed it to me with eyebrows furrowed -- he was obviously puzzled and none too pleased with the results.

I was then eating rhubarb pie (which I set aside). I took the reading glasses which were dangling on a chain from my neck and perused the paper he had shoved under my nose. Before I could even get past his name on the sheet, the forkful of pie I had set aside disappeared into his own mouth!

"It says here your verbal skills are exceptionally high and your math skills are good enough to get you into any college of your choice – just don't apply to MIT." I put the paper down on the tabletop, in front of him and took from him what was left of the pie.

"I got that. That's not the problem,' he said. He took the paper and pointed to the bottom portion. "Look at this."

"Possible career choices: newscaster, spokesperson, professor of literature, minister of the gospel, counselor or therapist – what's wrong with that?" I was beginning to think he just wanted my pie.

"Look at this – it says 'salesman'! What, me, a salesman?"

I suppose, like me, my son had a picture in his head of the average door-to-door salesman, pounding pavements, wearing a cheap suit shiny at the seams from having been pressed too many times, well-worn and scuffed shoes and lugging a valise that contained all his wares. That used to be the mental image of a salesman – in the 1930s, perhaps. The kind of salesman who got doors slammed in his face all the time.

There's another mental picture of a salesman that kind of turns the stomach. In our heads, we see a balding man reeking of hair pomade, wearing a plaid suit over a Hawaiian print shirt; fingers sporting an assortment of gold rings and one gold-capped tooth. When we think of a salesman, we think of a used car salesman – the one who could sell you a lemon as fast as he would sell you his shirt. When we see a salesperson like this, we cross to the other side of the street.

Then again, often, we have an image of the snobby salesclerk in a fancy boutique who wears the designer clothes that he sells. He looks like a supermodel but instead works on a commission off of the clothes he sells to middle-aged balding men in the throes of midlife crisis. He earns his living fawning like a sycophant reminiscent of the ministers of the Emperor who wore no clothes. Worse, if the salesman were a she, she'd look down her nose at you and tell you that you probably can't afford that purse you were looking at. We clearly stay away from those salespersons at all costs.

WE ARE ALL SALESMEN, whether we admit it or not. We sell ourselves and our ideas all the time to others. Often, we 'sell' ourselves without thinking twice about it – to a would-be employer, to would-be friends and would-be lovers.

Take the mother who tries to make her toddler eat his carrots and beans. She sits with him and eats the vegetables herself, smacking her lips and radiating joy and ecstasy with every bite of mushy boiled vegetable. She then plays with the food on the spoon, pretending it's a choo-choo train or a rocket ship. It works! The toddler opens his mouth and eats that mushy spoonful.

Take the teenager who is asking his mother to buy him a new stereo for his room or a new MP3 player, or a new smart phone (name it, kids want it) and they can sell their parents on the idea of buying it for them. They tell their parents: if you buy me a cell phone, you'd know where I am all the time because there will be GPS. You can send me messages to remind me to do my homework. I won't borrow you phone all the time. And they talk us into buying them the phones they want. Kids are born salesmen.

Take the coach who is trying to motivate his team into doing their best for the last do or die match of the season. He is pitching to them the idea that they can win if they work together and apply all that they have learned in training and all that they have experienced the whole season. He is trying to get them to believe in themselves and how they have what it takes to actually go out there, play hard, (get hurt, probably) and win. Coaches are salesmen.

Take the teacher who is trying to teach children the value of recycling and reducing their carbon footprints by segregating their trash and making money off of materials that can still be recycled. She makes them see a vision of the dire consequences if they fail or refuse to recycle. She then makes them see a vision of lush forests, purple mountains and clean clear air. The next thing you know, those kids are teaching their parents the value of recycling, too.

Take the supermodel who struts on the runway. The way she walks, smiles, turns and carries herself with confidence is selling an idea to all the other women like this: buy this dress and look beautiful, just like me. Supermodels are salespersons, too. They sell the ideal of beauty.

Take that guy at the office who wants to go out with the newly-hired office clerk. He smiles at her, strikes up a conversation with her, tries to be polite to her, trying to give her the lay of the land on the complicated power relationships at the office. He's actually doing all this because he is selling himself to her. He wants to put her at ease in his company so that he can ask her out. He is selling himself. Later, when he's been going out with her for a while, he will probably get down on his knee with a small velvet box in hand. He's not really just asking her to marry him, he's asking her to buy into a dream of living happily ever after.

Perhaps the greatest salesmen on earth are politicians running for office. They have got down the idea of salesmanship down to a formula. They dress like common folk; they pump hands and kiss babies; they eat pie and hold aloft a pig at county fairs. They sell the idea that they are just like you and me and they know what you and I want or need. They sell the idea that no one else can represent us or work for our benefit than them. Come election day we vote them into office! Politicians are the best salesmen of all. They are such good salesmen, we vote them into office again and again.

Guess what, even I – yes, the writer of this ebook, I am a salesman, too. I am selling to you the idea that you are already a salesman and you just don't know it. I'm trying to show you that you are just like the other millions on earth who pitch an idea to someone every day. You pitch to your kids the idea that it would be better for them to clean their room than to be grounded for a week. You pitch your husband the idea that it would be better if he fixes the leaky faucet himself than pay a plumber an arm and a leg and wait for him to come by your house after three weeks to fix it.

You pitch the idea to your girlfriends that trying a new diet or a new workout will improve your relationship with your husbands and bring more romance into your life. You pitch the idea to your boss that you are worth the raise you are asking for. You pitch the idea to your team how this new project can boost sales. You pitch ideas all the time. You try to persuade people to see your point of view about something. You gather and line up your best arguments that show how so much better their lives could be if they subscribe to your idea, your way of seeing things, your way of doing things. You are a salesman, no doubt about it – you just don't know it yet. And I suppose this is the main idea of this book. Everyone is already a salesman in theory and in everyday practice. Once you realize this, you can probably be motivated and emboldened to be a salesman by profession as well.

The most difficult part, in all human endeavors, is getting an idea fixed in your mind. And this is where it all starts. Once you realize that you have all that you need in order to sell something, you can work your way around most of the obstacles that your mind can foresee.

Where do we begin?

We begin with you and within you -- that is where this should all begin. Exactly who are you? What are your strengths and what are your weaknesses? What are your interests and what things get you all excited?

At the beginning, it would do you well to take pen and paper. Fold the paper lengthwise into two. Put on the top, by the left hand portion: 'The me I like' and on the top right hand portion, write: 'The me others like'. Then proceed to list down the traits and activities, characteristics, behavior and even physical, psychological, emotional and spiritual attributes you possess that you like and that others like about you.

The product of this list is your core capital in salesmanship. It is your view of yourself and your view of how others perceive you. This idea and picture you have of yourself colors every single thought you have; it tints every word you say; and it certainly gives flavor and texture to all that you do. It is your idea of who you are.

The next thing that you have to do is to decide, you have to figure out if you like this idea of who you are, if you are content with who you are and with how others perceive you. If you are not content, well, then, the dissatisfaction you feel will also color your thoughts, it will tint every word and it will give flavor and texture to all that you do. Dissatisfaction with ourselves is always the culprit that robs us of our confidence. It robs us of the freedom to be ourselves.

While we are on the subject, then, perhaps it would also be a good idea to make a list on the back of that piece of paper you had written all those things you like about yourself and those things other people like about you. The list on the back should be 'what I don't quite like about myself' and 'what others don't quite like about me'.

In case you were thinking that this exercise is just a bashing of your ego – it is not. Listing these things down as objectively and as truthfully as you can will give you a balanced view of yourself. Sticking to only those traits and characteristics that you like and adore about yourself will probably make you an egoist. And if you only think of yourself in terms of what is good about yourself, you might turn into an egotist!

Egoist and egotist

There is a difference, you know: an egoist is one concerned primarily with himself – how and what he feels, how and what he thinks. This is normal to the extent that we analyze how things from the outside (events, people) affect our inner well-being. It is an asset in salesmanship when because we are quick to pick up verbal cues and small facial expressions, we can read what people are saying and not saying. When we can 'read' people's reactions to us, to our product and to the way we talk, we are better able to tailor cut our pitch to suit the taste and preferences of the person we are talking to. Egoism, insofar as it helps us regulate our emotions, our emotional responses and motivations, can all be used to make us better salespersons.

An egotist, on the other hand, has no other concern but himself – he thinks about no one else but himself, he is full of himself – therefore, he can talk of nothing else but himself. The Good Book (The Holy Bible – the most ancient of all literature of wisdom) sums it up pretty well when it says: "Out of the abundance of the heart, the mouth speaketh." (Matthew 12:34). An egotist has no room in his affections, imaginations or actions for anyone or anything else but himself. Thus, he cannot be sensitive to how a potential customer feels – he cannot read the need of that person. He then cannot offer his product as an answer to that need.

The distinction makes an even bigger difference in that an egoist makes a better salesman. An egoist is a more perceptive and therefore a more flexible and intuitive salesperson. An egotist can never be a good salesperson – he is too full of himself to ever talk about a product outside of himself. Salesmanship involves selling a product by selling oneself and one's vision.

Compare your list with mine

In the next following pages we endeavor to make a list of the top ten traits that make a good salesperson. You can then compare your list with ours to see if you have the traits it takes to succeed in the profession of sales. There is a list of automatic negative thoughts that prevent you from being an effective salesperson and then there is a list of motivations that cause people to buy things.

The following lists are just my own. They are the traits that I find appealing in salespersons. They are the traits that a good salesperson has that help me decide to stop, look a product over, and buy it. I have not done any market research or psychological evaluation on this, just plain old common sense garnered from years of experience as a consumer who frequently shops for groceries, appliances and all the things I need for everyday living. I encounter salesclerks and salespeople all the time and I know what I like in them and what I don't like.

A good salesperson is warm but not overly familiar

Good manners are still the norm for salespersons. Saying 'good morning', 'good afternoon' and 'good evening' are still the way to go. A sincere smile with a sincere 'How may I help you today?' can get a conversation going with the walk-in customer at your shop.

If you are approaching a person who is strolling in the mall, a smile, a firm handshake and a brief introduction of yourself can set a good atmosphere. If you follow this with 'May I have a few minutes of your time to tell you about ___?' If you are met with a refusal, you can always smile and say,' it's just for a few minutes. Please?'

People often forget to make the magic words 'please' and 'thank you' part of their general vocabulary. It works wonders especially when it is sincerely said. If the customer is gruff, remember, he may be gruff, but his money is friendly. If you succeed in selling your product to this gruff customer it would be a great victory, indeed.

A good salesperson is congenial but not obsequious

Most salespeople look at potential customers only as potential customers. They forget that the potential customer is also a human being who warms up when they meet people who, like them, are civilized human beings ready and willing to interact meaningfully with each other. Potential customers are not prey and sales persons are not predators who are looking for the fool from whom he can wrest his money.

Salesmanship should be an honorable profit-making profession. Customers are people with needs and you, as a salesperson is someone who can meet that need. The soonest you can identify what the person's need is, the faster you can throw a good light on yourself and your product as the means to meet the customer's needs.

You can ask questions without being intrusive; you can be helpful and make suggestions without being insistent. You can do all this if you look at the potential customer as a person just like you, only with money to spend on something he needs or wants. Your speech must always be gracious, well-seasoned to meet the customer's expectations.

A good salesperson is presentable but not intimidating

As a salesperson, you have to bring identification. Some wear a uniform with the company logo that not only identifies them with the company's reputation it also convinces the potential buyer that you are a person whom they can safely speak with as you are not planning a home invasion.

You must dress appropriately. If you are selling life insurance, you must dress smartly and in be in business attire because insurance sales are a serious business proposition. If you are a party planner who sells party packages for children, you must wear clothes that exude fun and bring samples of the party favors and pictures of other parties you have organized and planned. If you are selling a credit card product, you must dress the part of the market niche you are trying to reach: if your credit card has freebies for female yuppies (young, upwardly mobile urban professional), then you must dress as a yuppy as well.

Dressing appropriately lets the potential customer know that you, just like them, have identical needs and wants, therefore, your opinion can be trusted when you suggest that they invest their hard-earned money in buying your product.

People usually desire to conform to standards. And they presume that others do, too. Thus, dressing in a manner that conforms to standards of a certain business will give a common starting point on which a conversation can begin and a sales pitch can be founded upon.

A good salesperson is enthusiastic but not overwhelming

Zest for living is contagious. If you are a salesperson and you cannot be enthusiastic about introducing your product to people or introducing people to your product, then who else can be enthusiastic for your product? You will want people to think of your smiling face whenever they see the logo of your product. You will want them to remember your energy and your positive attitude toward your product, toward selling it and toward the customer.

There is precious little in this world to be happy about and so many things to be grumpy about instead. Thus, if you can find it in your mind to focus on something positive about yourself, about your product, about your customer or about life in general, then you have won half the battle.

You will want your attitude to help generate excitement about your product. The only way you can do this is by being enthusiastic about your product. Focus on the points that attract customers and those that make them something that people want to have. They are your natural selling points. Be enthusiastic about that because there are so many other products out there and if you can be enthusiastic about your product, it will help sell the idea that your product is probably the best of the bunch.

A good salesperson is articulate but not talkative

The point in you being the salesperson for your particular product is that you are your product's spokesperson, endorser and satisfied customer. There is a presumption that you know all about your product so that you can answer the simplest questions a potential buyer would have about it. It is no good for you to try to sell a product without knowing what it is. The first rule of sales, I suppose, is: know your product. If you do not know your product, if you do not know its specifications, if you don't know how to use it, how can you sell it?

Buyers always want to know: Does it work? That is the most basic question they have in their minds even if they do not say it out loud. How does it work? It the next question that comes to their mind. Out loud, the customer or buyer would probably ask questions like: Does it run on batteries? What kind of batteries would I need? Does it come with a charger? How long do I have to charge it? These are important questions, but not only because you can converse with the customer about the product, but because you can use those questions to actually address the customer's unspoken concerns about buying your product.

The most logical unspoken concern of a buyer is: how does this thing work, anyway? The customer doesn't want to appear stupid. But he really wants to know how your product works. Which button should I press to turn it on? This is probably the question the buyer wants to know as he turns the product over and inspects it. While ostensibly seeming interested in the specifications, the buyer is actually asking you: Can you show me how to use it? These are questions that an interested buyer is itching to ask of a salesperson.

I remember seeing a sign that announced a sale on digital cameras. The specifications on the poster (the number of pixels — 16 mega pixels - whatever they are) told me that this is the kind of camera I wanted to get for my daughter. It announced great features but was it simple enough for a 14 year old to operate? Heck, was it simple enough for me to operate? Was it powerful enough to suit my daughter's needs to document her life and activities but not too flashy so as to invite a mugging?

I didn't know anything about digital cameras. The last time I bought a camera for myself, it was the kind that needed 35mm film that had to be loaded and winded up, and it used alkaline batteries for the flash and timer. I don't know where to insert the memory card on a digital camera. I didn't know which button to use for the zoom, the flash of the effects.

The salesclerk saw my discomfort and apparent panic. She smiled at me and said, 'Ma'am, are you buying this for yourself or as a gift?' When I said it was a gift to give to a teenager, she said 'Teenagers can work anything technical. But just so you can be sure that this camera works, let me show you how to use it.' She showed me how to load the batteries, the memory card and to point and shoot. She showed me the flashing little red light that signaled that the camera was ready to be used.

That got my motor going and she encouraged me to take a shot of anything in the store. She then showed me how to work the video camera, the flash, the zoom and the effects. She allowed me to take a few pictures and showed me how to look at the pictures in the memory card and delete the ones that weren't any good.

By the time she had finished showing me how that camera worked, she didn't have to sales talk me into anything. I was so raring to try using the camera myself. I entered that particular store because of a poster that showed a camera within my price range. I came in still unsure if the camera that was on sale was the camera I wanted. After the salesclerk demonstrated it to me, I was sure that it was a camera I wanted because I can work it! I don't think I ever gave that particular camera to my daughter at all – that camera is in my purse! So you see, I ended up buying two cameras that day: one for myself (a sleek red one) and another one for my daughter (a black one because she's into black these days).

A good salesperson is knowledgeable but not a know-it-all

In that same example above, the salesclerk could have tried to impress me with f-stops and lens apertures and pixels and resolutions. She did not. She saw my obvious (middle-aged person's) fear of technology and she showed me how to take a picture with that device. She didn't have to teach me how it was made or where it was made or by whom it was made. She relied upon the integrity and goodwill of the telecommunications company that manufactured the camera. She presumed that I didn't need to know everything about the camera or that I wanted to know all about digital photography. She could tell I just needed to know how to turn it on, point it, aim it and shoot it and then to be able to see the picture that I had just taken. She presumed right, too.

She didn't think I was too stupid to learn it so she didn't 'talk down to me'. She didn't think I was probably knowledgeable all about cameras. And watch me make a fool of myself trying to turn that camera on. She showed me how to use the camera and the demonstration itself sold the camera to me. It was user-friendly. She showed me that it was user-friendly, she didn't just tell me. That made her, in my book, a good salesperson. She made an impression on me with her no-nonsense demonstration and all the while, she didn't try to impress me at all.

A good salesperson is patient but not a doormat

Once in a while, there are customers who are sarcastic and crude. They use words to pick a product apart, trying to discover its weaknesses and its shortcomings so that he can haggle for a lower price, or maybe the customer had a bad day at the office and is taking out his stress on a salesclerk. Whatever the customer's psychological workings are, here is the customer who seems hell bent on insulting the product but ends up insulting you, the salesperson as well.

A good salesperson can respond graciously, with a smile, and treat the customer as though he were a spoiled and petulant child: disregard the insulting tone and still engage the customer in a sober conversation about the product.

When the customer raises a point about the product's shortage of features a wise salesperson will not argue. He will instead agree in part with the customer pointing out that the features that the customer wants can be found in a pricier product (which she is perfectly willing to show him) while emphasizing that the product before them at the moment delivers exactly what it promises, although its features are few.

In fact, if you take the customer on and cater to his need for the more advanced features, you can actually sell him a pricier product precisely because he is in search of a particular feature or specification that cannot be delivered by a budget-friendly or more economical product. Often, the customer feels that since he had dug his heels and harped on an expensive feature, he cannot back out now when the pricier brand and model is shown to him just as he desires.

The customer won't feel insulted at all because you totally agree with him. If you can inject a bit of wit and humor, you may even coax the customer out of his bad humor. You can probably say that the advanced features he is looking for is specific only to a patented brand. You can agree with him that it is a really good feature and it shows his good taste to seek to purchase a product with such an advanced feature.

You can always turn it around. You don't have to take a customer's insults lying down like a doormat, use it as a sales pitch. Use his insults to paint him into a corner so that he can put his money where his mouth is.

A good salesperson is diligent and hardworking

A good salesperson must be diligent and hardworking. He has to find buyers. He has to drum up interest in his product. So the salesperson is always trying to find ways to showcase his product and trying to find opportunities to tell people all about it.

Buyers don't always walk into your store. Often, you have to work hard to induce them to come it or to entice them to come in. Sometimes, you don't have a store – sometimes, you have to go into people's homes or offices, meet them where they are at and make a sales pitch right there and then. To do this, you would have to go up to the potential customer with or without a referral or an introduction.

When you do have a referral or an introduction, you would still need to research that person's particular needs and preferences before giving your presentation. If you want to give a spectacular presentation, you need to work hard on a Powerpoint presentation or create a leaflet or a handout.

You also have to do a lot of market research. You need to know what kind of buyers would be interested in your product and where these buyers may be found. If you were selling double fried chicken from a food truck, then all you have to do is find a sporting or other social event where you can park your truck and proceed to sell from the parking space you found.

If you are selling time shares in a condominium at a holiday destination, you probably have to go to that holiday destination and set up a booth or a desk at local hotels. Your selling point would be, why spend for a cramped hotel room when you can own a time share in a condominium where your whole family can stay? These are potential buyers who have the money to spend for a holiday time share. These are buyers who have the lifestyle that involves travelling. It will be like catching fish from a barrel. Just the same, though, you would have to set up a booth, research on the best time to throw your net to get maximum results (that should be the height of summer which is the peak season for travelling).

A successful salesperson is necessarily one who is unafraid of hard work. Success in the field of sales requires a lot of hard work. So if you are not ready or single-minded about giving a hundred per cent effort to make a sale, then you ought to find another job.

A good salesperson must be imaginative and intuitive

In order to make a good sales presentation, you must be imaginative. You must be able to walk in your buyer's shoes a bit and see how it would feel like. You must see your product from their perspective before you can hope to find a way to pitch your product to them.

If, as in the example above, you were selling a time share in a condominium at a holiday destination, you have to look at the buyer's family because they are the ones who will definitely benefit from such an investment. You can tell your buyer who may be a father with kids that he can spend more time with his kids on the beach instead of trying to find a hotel that can accommodate all of you. He can take your kids to the local market, buy the local produce, make breakfast or lunch for them instead of paying for room service so that you can really bond with your family.

You can think ahead and allow your imagination (as well as the buyer's imagination) to run for a bit to his child's graduation – a two week vacation would be a worthwhile gift for his son who graduated with honors. Or, his daughter can have her sweet sixteen or debut at the beach with her friends and they can all stay in the time-share condominium. She can even have her wedding on the beach and still use the time-share.

Projecting how a product can appreciate in value or make a return on the initial investment is one great way to make the buyer make an investment in your product. You need imagination and intuition for this. You have to be able to 'read' the buyer's priorities and his values so that you can make the product more attractive to him.

A good salesperson is persuasive but not overbearing

No one wants a hard sell. First, a hard sell creates pressure on a buyer. Second, pressure can easily be interpreted as undue influence. Third, you may have succeeded in selling a product to a particular customer but the customer's experience because of the hard sell was rather painful for him, not enjoyable at all. Fourth, because of the hard sell, he will not be able to recommend you to his friends or relatives. This way, you made one sale instead of making one sale and three other potential sales.

A good sale is one that appeals to the buyer's reason, emotions and will. Appeal to his reason by showing him that your product is worth his attention and investment. Appeal to his emotions by showing him how the product can help him live up to his life's values and priorities. Appeal to his will by encouraging him to 'make a small investment'.

Always refer to a purchase as an investment for the buyer because it is. What for you is a sale is an investment for the buyer who buys the product. By buying your product, he makes an investment in a vision or a lifestyle that the product promotes. It is an investment in a relationship with a product and with its representative – you, the salesperson.

A good salesperson is genuine with a genuine story

There was this lady who when we were small children, was working part-time to put herself through school. She came to the house after her classes and she would help clean the house, do chores and help with the kids. She was nice to the kids and the kids missed her when she had finished her studies and went away to find a job.

Years later, I met her again (at church, of all places). She began going to the same church my family and I went to. My mother who helped put her through school was overjoyed to see her. I was beginning to wonder why she had gone back to see us. We invited her to our house for lunch and after the meal, she cornered my mother and began showing her bottles of massage oils. She was selling them. My mother bought two bottles for old time's sake and she left. We didn't see her for a spell.

Later, she came back to the house, this time, she was selling a different brand of massage oils. This time, though, she claimed that this particular brand of massage oil can cure rheumatism, it can get rid of toxins (and on and on, ad nauseam). My mother bought two bottles for old time's sake. And thus it began. We wouldn't see her for a spell and then she'd turn up selling a different brand of massage oils. She then branched out and began selling vitamin supplements. My mother would buy a token amount from her time and time again.

I left for college; I went and got myself a job; I got married and had my own kids, and this lady keeps showing up at our doorstep every few months with new products to sell. She doesn't get it. People do not buy from her except out of pity. They buy from her because it is better to buy from her than for them to lend or give her money. She cannot sell more than a few bottles of massage oil to anyone in particular. This is because she is just peddling them. What sets apart a good salesperson from a common street peddler is one's belief in the superiority of his product.

Contrast this lady with a lady I once met on a metro. I knew her because our kids went to the same school. The ride was long and we were both seated. She and I got to talking. She remarked that she hadn't been seeing a lot of me at the kids' school and I said that I hadn't been feeling well. I had symptoms of ulcer. She listened intently as I described my symptoms and she said that she had the same symptoms years before. She began telling me of how she went from doctor, trying antacid after antacid and other medications. She underwent an endoscopy and the results were normal. She had gone through a battery of tests, too, just like me.

Then, she said, she read a newspaper article about another woman who had similar symptoms. That newspaper article told her of a natural health food supplement made from aloe vera. Aloe vera, she told me, was used to treat cuts and burns. The same principle applied when aloe vera was taken as a food supplement. She gave me a sample. She said that she was a direct seller of this food supplement. She gave me a testimonial. She was, in fact, on the metro because she was going to see her sister-in-law who was experiencing the same gastric symptoms. I took the sample and I did feel relief. I called her and bought a few bottles. The few bottles became a regular thing until all the gastric symptoms disappeared. Today, I would recommend the same aloe vera food supplement to anyone who told me that they had the same gastric symptoms.

The difference between this woman and my mother's student was that one believed in the superiority of her product and she had a personal story to back up her belief. Her story is validated by botanical science (aloe vera is an effective first aid cure for burns). Most importantly, her story and her sales pitch were validated by her own personal experience in using the product. She is a good salesperson and spokesperson and endorser for that aloe vera food supplement.

Common automatic negative thoughts that keep you from being an effective salesperson

It's embarrassing. If you think about sales as twisting people's arms to buy a product they neither need nor want, then you should be embarrassed. But if you think of sales as meeting people's legitimate although unspoken or unrecognized needs, then, you are actually helping people meet their needs. What is so embarrassing about that? An insurance agent sells a sense of security. A realtor sells a dream of home and family. A car salesman is selling not only a means of transportation but also a status symbol, a tool of a trade and a lifestyle upgrade.

They won't believe me. If you prepare yourself by knowing your product then there is no reason why you shouldn't be credible and believable. You can prepare by asking yourself what a possible questions an interested buyer may have. You can also brainstorm by listing down possible objections people can have about your product. If what you are selling is something that requires a big cash outlay, you can team up with a financing corporation such as a bank so that those who wish to buy your product but may need funding can have recourse. You may even include as part of your service the processing of your client's mortgage or financing plan. This can be further marketed as a total product package.

I don't talk so good. A salesperson's capital is not only his appearance, it is also his speech. It is your words that will make the buyer sit up and listen to what you have to say. It is your delivery of those words that will convince them that your product is a good investment for their money. If you are insecure about your grammar or your pronunciation, then you must improve this daily. Learn one new word everyday and use the words you've learned in sentences. Work on the structure of the sentences until they sound right.

You must read, read, read! Read newspapers and magazines that will not only expand your vocabulary but also expand your views, your perspectives and help you brush up on current events. Some current events are crucial in closing a sale. For instance, if your buyer has a husband or wife working in the Middle East, any war or armed conflict in that area may delay financial transactions that may cause your buyer to default on a payment.

You must not only read, you must also read out loud so that you can hear yourself. You must listen to good speakers (such as news casters) and analyze what makes them good speakers. Most people will tell you that an effective speaker is one who gets his point across and does so in a manner that is convincing in its genuineness. All good public speakers will tell you that confidence and conviction always count more than one's pronunciation or grammar.

No one will listen to me or give me the time of day. If you stop a random stranger on the street then that random stranger will probably walk on by, totally ignoring you. This is understandable as people are wary of strangers, especially those who shove brochures in their face or attempt to be so friendly and so familiar so soon. Learn to cultivate contacts and to build your network. Have business cards made. Begin with people you know. Get out your rolodex, your little black book, the car pool directory, the PTA directory and even the church directory. If your relatives, friends and acquaintances are not interested in buying from you, then you can probably mine them for referrals. They must know someone who is interested in buying your product. You may even prevail upon them to accompany you and introduce you to the person they referred you to. In this way, you will not be approaching the prospective buyer as a stranger – you are a friend of a friend.

I don't know anyone who wants to buy it. You wouldn't know if any of your relatives, friends and acquaintances is interested in buying your product until you actually talk to them about your product. Do not say that none of them is interested until you have actually asked them for an appointment and actually sat down with them and presented to them your product. Don't miss out on an opportunity to find a buyer by automatically telling yourself that no one is interested even before you have actually spoken to them and they have slammed a door on your face.

I can't bully people. Only mobsters bully people into buying products they do not want or need. Only shysters defraud others, saddling them with onerous payments for products they cannot benefit from. The best salespersons are able to perceive people's needs and match them with products that meet those needs. A good salesperson knows his product inside out that he can find people who need his products. The best salespersons value people as people and not as walking and breathing pocketbooks or ATM cards.

The best salespersons listen to other people as they articulate their hopes, dreams and aspirations and frame their sales pitch with these hopes, dreams and aspirations in mind. No force, undue pressure, misrepresentations, insidious machinations or shenanigans are needed to bully or persuade people to buy your products. Find what motivates them and frame your presentation to address those motivations – the buyers will line up to buy your products – all you will need to do is issue a sales receipt.

I don't know anything about sales. It's not really salesmanship that you need to be informed about in order to make a sale. What you need to be is observant about people's buying habits. Who had the bright idea of putting a magazine stand at the grocery store check-out counter? I'll tell you who: it was that person who observed that people waiting for their turn to pay for their groceries would probably be bored just standing there. Having a magazine stand next to the cash register will give them something to read within those few minutes that they wait. And their interest in reading the magazines may actually lead them to put the magazine in their cart and buy it so that they can read at home the entire article that they began reading while standing at the check-out counter.

What you need to be is observant about people's values and priorities. A woman who totes around an expensive designer bag may be interested in purchasing products that enhance their status symbol. Thus, any product that will tend to enhance their feeling that they have 'arrived' will be attractive to them: the latest smart phone, the latest tablet personal computer, the latest model and make of an expensive car or even a fine Swiss-made watch.

I don't know anything about rocket science. You don't have to have a particular IQ level to be a good salesperson. What you do need is a lot of street 'smarts'. You must know how to talk at your prospective buyer's level. If your prospective buyer is a married professional woman, then you must talk to her at her level and present your products in a manner that appeals to their reason. If your prospective buyer is a single young urban professional then you have to present them with products that fit their lifestyle.

You don't have to be a genius. You don't have to be philosophical. You don't have to be intellectual. All you have to know is all that there is to know about your products. You need to know which features of your products to highlight in your presentation so that the prospective buyer's needs and motivations are reached by your presentation.

If you are selling magazine subscriptions for example, it would help you to know if your prospective buyer is a math or a language teacher so that you can put together a package of subscriptions to magazines that can enhance her teaching. If your prospective is a techie, you can put together a package that includes science magazines, computer magazines and applied mechanics magazines. If your prospective buyer owns a salon, then the package you offer the salon owner has a lot of clothing and make-up articles, glossy magazines that have pictures of models and celebrities with different hairstyles. You have to know all about your buyer and all about your product so that you can aptly match your products to your buyer's tastes.

It's dangerous. Any business activity carries with it a certain amount of risk. Can you avoid risk altogether? Probably not, but you can be prepared when they do crop up. If you are worried about the sales contract you are asking your buyer to sign, get an appointment with a lawyer and ask him to explain to you your rights and obligations under that contract. If you are worried about loss, get insurance. If you are worried over theft, install an alarm system.

If you are worried about competition, then make sure you innovate. It is not enough to sell good products you must also learn how to package your products: be innovative. You can give small freebies or gifts, a rebate or a discount when their purchase reaches a certain amount. You can give them coupons that they can use on their next purchase. You can offer your products on a buy-one-get-one basis. You can even include a discounted price on a small item that can be used with the product they just bought. For example, if they buy a washer and dryer, include a flat iron for half the price. The flat iron is necessarily used when people do their own laundry at home. If you are selling a car, why not include a tire inflator? Every car owner and driver experiences a flat tire. A tire inflator will be attractive to a person who is buying a car.

They'll laugh at me. You will be in good company. They laughed at Copernicus, at Galileo and Leonardo da Vinci. The people in their time thought they were good-for-nothing dreamers and ne'er do well. What they did not know was that they will be vindicated by history. And after they were dead, they were hailed as innovators and great thinkers.

Who would have thought that an old soldier who had a good recipe for fried chicken can one day own an international franchise? He wanted to start his own restaurant but he had no money and no interested investors in his restaurant idea. What he did was he travelled all around the country and went into diners and greasy spoons. He offered to teach them how to make his tasty chicken. Right in front of them, he made his chicken. He served it to them and boy, did they love his chicken. The next thing he did was he sold them the recipe for the chicken and the right to make the chicken using his recipe. Voila, the most popular chicken fast food franchise was born. To others in his time, he must have looked a bit crazy, traipsing all over creation cooking chicken for strangers. Today, everyone knows his chicken. Don't worry about people laughing at you – they won't be laughing when you are laughing all the way to the bank because all your hard work and creativity has at last paid off.

Defining need: inner motivations for buying activities

When I was little, my mother used to give me a small weekly allowance. When she put the money in my hand, she would hold my hand in both her hands, look at me straight in the eye and say 'Buy what you need, not what you want'. Back then, I didn't get it. I always thought I needed candy. I needed it to make me feel good after eating a plateful of vegetables. I always bought pop because it kept me sane after my mother forced me to drink milk.

When the allowance was all gone, my mother would ask me if I had saved any of the allowance she gave me. I'd shake my head. She'd ask me how much of it was still left and I'd just hang my head. She would always say that a 'need' is something that you cannot do without; a 'want' is everything else. A 'need' is something that you require to reach a goal, a want is something you desire to own or possess. It took me years to understand the difference.

There are a lot of adults out there who still have not figured out the difference between a want and a need. There are others who have a lot of disposable income that they can acquire all their needs and still have a lot left over to also acquire their wants.

In order to be a good salesperson, you must learn how to identify people's needs and wants. People's needs and wants may be unspoken. They may not even be aware of their inner needs and wants. You must learn to perceive these and frame the presentation of your products to meet those needs and to cater to those wants.

Some people have specific needs. There are products that do not need to be presented to buyers as the products already cater to specific needs. For instance, prescription eyeglasses are products that people suffering from myopia or presbyopia will buy. You do not need to talk them into buying prescription eyeglasses they will buy them regularly once or twice every year. Shades used to be a fashion accessory but now with the ozone layer depleted and the sun's ultraviolet rays stronger than ever, shades and sun glasses are no longer mere fashion accessories, they are needs. People will buy prescription glasses and shades.

The only question for them is the cost and the style of the prescription glasses or shades. Thus, if you sell prescriptive eyeglasses, you must have in stock prescriptive eyeglasses of all shapes, sizes and prices to suit each buyer's capacity to pay. You can sell designer brands, you can sell those made of titanium alloy or you can sell ordinary frames made of plastic. You can sell glass lenses, plastic lenses, lenses that change color with the amount of light available, ultrathin lenses, lenses that have UV protection or antiglare, lenses that are scratch proof. People will buy them.

What will set you apart from other stores selling prescription glasses will be the price, the availability of stocks and the free eye refraction. You can also make sure that the prescription glasses are ready in an hour – this service would corner the market of those who need emergency replacement for glasses that just broke or got lost.

Some need a product for a lifestyle upgrade. A newly married couple who each own a small subcompact sedan may need to buy a bigger car that can accommodate a car seat once they are expecting their first baby. If they are expecting their second or third child, they will need a minivan so that they can accommodate as many car seats and as many accessories such as strollers, portable cribs, playpens and diaper bags.

In the same token, a newly married couple living in a studio apartment may need to buy a bigger apartment with two or three bedrooms to accommodate their first baby. A family expecting their third or fourth child will probably move from an apartment to a bungalow with a front yard and a back yard so that the kids can have a place to play and explore.

These people will buy these products not because they want them but they need them for the new lifestyle that they are sporting. With an increase in income, there is also an increase in spending. It is what drives the economy. People spending money drives the wheels of the economy. More spending increases demand for products and increased demand for products will spur an increase creation of products.

No other example more vividly illustrates this than the buying spree that the Chinese are experiencing right now. The higher their productivity rises, the higher their demand for goods increases. Designer brands are setting up shop in China because the newly affluent Chinese want to buy them. The Chinese are trading in their bicycles and scooters for German luxury car brands. Increased wealth brings increased spending.

Some need status symbols. A person who had just been promoted at work may need a new car, a new cell phone, a new personal computer. Buying and acquiring more expensive and high-end products reflect the rise in his status at work. In the end, the increase in income must be accompanied by evidence of an increased power to purchase. Getting a promotion does not only mean a higher income, it also means more responsibility, and more power. The acquisition of power must be accompanied by symbols that befit the new financial and career status. For example, the promotion at work requires a new wardrobe that speaks of his new position of power. The new wardrobe is justified because as a manager, he will have to attend more meetings with the bosses who are in the upper echelons of power in the company. There will be more cocktails, soirees and public relations functions to attend.

A change in civil status from single to married or from married to divorced or from married to widowed will also require new status symbols to correspond to the change in civil status. A single person would need to buy a new bed, stove, refrigerator and home furnishings. A newly divorced person would need a smaller home, a smaller bed, a smaller refrigerator and less ostentatious furnishings.

They need a product to feel good about themselves. A woman who has just ended up a long-term relationship may buy a whole new wardrobe to feel like a new person. Her old clothes were all associated with memories (both good and bad) from the former relationship and she wants to feel like a whole new person in order to move on with her new single life.

A newly retired professional may consider selling the big house where he raised his family and move into a new condominium he had just purchased with his retirement pay. His children may have all finished college and are now living in different cities. He may want to indulge a passion he has been saving up for so long – travelling the world over. For this he would need to buy air line tickets, cruise ship tickets and new luggage. He would also need a new insurance policy so that he can have protection for his loved ones. Travelling was something he had always wanted to do but had no time for when he was working, building his career, paying mortgage, saving for his kids' college fund, and raising a family. Now that he has retired, he has the time to what he has always wanted to do. This new activity will make him feel good about retiring.

Retirement often brings depression because of the sudden cessation of your usual activities. For people whose jobs gave them a lot of satisfaction, losing the job means losing a lot of satisfaction with life that work afforded. If the retiree cultivated deep lasting friendships at work, retirement will spell a loss of some meaningful relationships. Something must fill up the void that work used to fill. Travelling around the world may fill that void and bring satisfaction.

Other retirees invest their hard-earned retirement pay into a new business or career. Some would get further education or training. Some would try writing. All these new activities will spur on buying activities. You will do well to take advantage of this buying activity.

They just want it. Some people are not afraid of owning up to their desires. They know what they want and they just go and get it. Some people see a new product or an old one that to them is interesting and they buy it for the sheer pleasure of owning it. Some art collectors behave this way. To them a work of art is an investment in the finer things in life. They want a painting and it does not matter if it is made by a new or unknown artist or an established artist. Some even purchase classic works of art. Collecting art is their passion and they indulge their passion. Some people collect art as a financial investment – the work of art appreciates in value in time. They can turn it into cash or they can donate it to a museum. The museum will keep the work of art for other generations to enjoy.

If you think about owning a work of art entails additional expense. A collector would need to purchase insurance to protect the works of art. He would need temperature or climate control in the place where he will store the work of art. Anyone who indulges a passion for art and purchases works of art must be purchasing it simply because they want it.

These are just some of the reasons why people purchase products. These are their motivations for buying things. To be able to perceive a prospective buyer's motivations for buying is a skill worth gaining if you want to be a successful salesperson.

What should you sell?

Now that you have finally believed that you have the capacity and the ability to be a successful salesperson, the next logical question is, what can you sell? What should you sell?

You can join the bandwagon and take advantage of market trends. If stiletto heels are the thing, consider selling designer stiletto heels. If you are thinking big, you can actually set up a company that sells made-to-order stiletto heels that match the fabric of dresses. A customer sends in a picture of a dress or outfit that needs matching shoes and you create the matching stiletto heels for the dress.

The only problem with this is that with each fashion season, the trends in shoes come and go. What is fashionable during one season may no longer be fashionable at the next fashion season. You can sell shoes if that is your passion but you may soon feel like a hamster on a wheel trying to keep up with new trends in shoes. If this is what excites you, then you should do it by all means.

What you should sell is a product that ignites your passion and keeps your interest burning. Find a product that tickles your fancy, one that makes your imagination run wild. Selling that product will be easier for you because you would know all about that product and your excitement and conviction will be palpable from every word you utter.

Sometimes, it takes a long time to find the product that will do justice to your salesmanship skills and abilities. Sometimes, because you need to make money, you will begin with selling things that you don't particularly fancy and while selling that, you come across other products. And these new products will become your passion.

A true story that I hope will inspire you

There was this woman who taught kids' Sunday School at her church. There she met the man whom she would marry. On weekdays, she would be on her sewing machine making clothes for her customers at her dress shop. On Saturdays, she would go around the poor neighborhood where they lived and she taught the kids songs, Bible verses, Bible stories and on Sundays, she picked up those kids and they walked to the church.

She did much the same thing after she had married her husband. Her husband taught kids' Sunday School at their church, too. On the weekdays, he was a beat cop who was studying hard to become a lawyer. When they had three children, her husband finally finished law school and passed the bar. He began working as a lawyer. He told his wife to quit working as a seamstress so that she can concentrate on raising the kids. After a while, two more kids were added to their family.

One day, her husband decided to run for public office. He did not win the election and had used up most of his savings. The wife decided to help her husband. She began selling homemade food she cooked. She would meet people around the neighborhood and sell to them her homemade baked goodies. She met someone who sold women's make-up. So she added that to the items she sold. She began selling the make-up and baked goodies at her friend's office. She collected payment for the items she sold every payday.

One day, as she was collecting payment, her friend had a visitor. The visitor was a real estate sales agent at a realty company. Her friend 's husband was working in the Middle East as an engineer and so they were thinking of investing his earnings by buying a house of their own. The lady visitor was offering her friend a house in a newly developed community. Before the lady visitor left, she gave her a business card and told her that when she got tired of selling make-up and baked goodies for a few dollars, she should call her and she will recruit her to be a t estate sales agent like her.

She thought she'd try it out and went to see the lady visitor. She was immediately recruited and was given a seminar on salesmanship. She was a wife and mother of five, she was 46 years old and she was one semester shy of graduating from college. She began her career in sales.

She was told that when she sold houses or condominiums, she wasn't really selling a house or a condominium she was selling a dream of a good life. The economy was good and she can sell houses and condominiums to people as an investment. Real property always appreciated in value. They can sell the property they had purchased at a later time if they had no interest in living in the house or condominium property they bought from her.

She began by selling those started houses to newlyweds. She got 1.25% of the purchase price of each house she sold. After she sold a few of those, she was advised by the same lady realtor who recruited her to recruit other sales agent like herself. And from their sales, she can get an override. Her commission from the sales of her recruits would be 2.5 %.

Slowly but surely, she began recruiting others as real estate agents. At the same time, she continued selling houses and condominiums. From being at the very bottom as a sales agent, she became a unit manager and then she became a branch manager. She was earning 5% off of the sales that the sales agents and unit managers under her and earning 7.5% off of each sale she made personally.

When the lady realtor took the real estate broker's examination and passed it, she left the realty company and joined a bigger realty company that developed and sold its own housing and condominium projects. She was pirated and was promoted to the position of Area Sales Director earning 10% off of the sales of the sales agents, unit managers and branch managers under her supervision. She was earning on two fronts: she earned by recruiting more salesmen and by training them and assisting them until they made their first sale. She was also earning by selling properties on her own.

By the time she was 60 years old, she was assistant vice president and she had a sales force of about 60 people under her supervision. She consistently recruited and trained sales people as well as consistently selling herself. By the time she retired at age 69, she had begun her own real estate sales company.

What lesson can you learn from her story?

It is never too late to begin a career in sales. If you have a knack for talking to people and connecting with them, you can have a career in sales. If you find a product that you can believe in, then you can be a successful salesperson.

That lady believed that every housewife can be a real estate sales agent. She told her recruits who were mostly stay-at-home moms like herself that they can first tap their family for referrals and then their friends. Their first sales were usually the house and lot bought by relative of theirs. She told them that they can sell in their spare time, while the kids were in school. She taught them how to talk to teachers and to other parents in their kids' schools and tap those contacts for referrals.

All that time, she talked to people and sold them their dream home. She sold them the wisest investment for their hard-earned money. With the money she made from real estate sales, she had helped put all her five kids through college. She was able to buy a car for her personal use and a van to use when she took her recruits on trips to see newly developed housing subdivisions that they had authority to sell. Later, she was able to buy her own dream home herself.

She believed in her product. She knew her product. She was able to convey to her buyers the need to invest their money in real property. She helped them secure mortgage loans, she helped them through documentation. After they had fully paid for the properties that they bought, she helped them transfer the title to their own name. She provided families with their own homes. She provided other women with a career in sales. She had taken in students who had run out of money to finance their college education. She taught them how to sell real estate and the money they earned helped in financing their college education. She took new graduates who could not yet find jobs and trained them in sales. By the time they finally got a call from the employers they had applied to, they were earning so much more in real estate sales than they would in an office job. Some took an office job so that they can have a regular income but dabbled in real estate sales using their office contacts as customers or tapping them for referrals. They made more money on the side than they ever did from their regular jobs.

All this, she did when she was 46 until she was 69. She inspired many by her hard work, her tenacity and her dedication. She inspired them to make something out of themselves and raise their family's income by going into sales. She empowered ordinary housewives so that they can have a career they can fall back on in case they were separated or divorced or widowed.

All this time, she still taught Sunday School at church every Sunday. You know how I know? She's my mom. Take it from me when I say that you can be a salesperson. You have to believe that you have it in you to talk to people and tell them all about this exciting product you have. You can tell them your story – how you found this product, how this product addressed your own need, how your life was changed by this product. Your personal story, your testimony will sell this product.

Find a product you can believe in because if you believe in the product you are selling, then you can sell it every day. Find the resolve to keep on keeping on until your diligent efforts have paid off. Yes, you can be a salesman. You can be a good salesman.

We Want Your Feedback on This Book!

Our main purpose is to make sure that our readers get value from the books we publish and that they have a good experience with all of our products. We are always working to improve our books and other products with every revision and update.

Every piece of feedback makes a difference in this process. And we would appreciate yours as well - whether it is good or bad.

Please take one minute to let us know what you thought by following this link:

http://checkmatemg.com/feedbackselling

www.ingramcontent.com/pod-product-compliance
Lightning Source LLC
Chambersburg PA
CBHW071824170526
45167CB00003B/1412